France

This book was devised and produced by
Multimedia Publications (UK) Ltd

Editor: Marilyn Inglis
Production: Karen Bromley
Design: John Strange and Associates
Picture Research: David Sutherland

First published in the United States of
America 1985 by Gallery Books, an imprint of
W. H. Smith Publishers Inc., 112 Madison
Avenue, New York, NY 10016

ISBN 0 8317 3543 0

Typeset by Flowery Typesetters Ltd
Origination by C.L.G. Verona
Printed in Italy by Sagdos, Milan

France

Rob Neillands

GALLERY BOOKS
An Imprint of W. H. Smith Publishers Inc.
112 Madison Avenue
New York City 10016

Endpapers A lavender farm in Provence.

Half Title page Burgundy vineyards under cultivation.

Title page Cows graze quietly as twilight comes to this peaceful Burgundy farm.

This page A typically French tree-lined avenue.

CONTENTS

White horses herded by *guardiens,* the cowboys of the Camargue, splash across the waters of the marshy delta.

CHAPTER 1

Hidden France

France is a country full of unexpected corners. As it is the largest country in Western Europe, and one with a long, fascinating and complicated history, this is hardly surprising. What *is* surprising is that so few travelers or tourists who flock into France each year take the trouble to stray far from their well-trodden tracks and see a little of those glories of France which are no less wonderful for being so little known. All it takes is a little time, and the will to wander.

Even in the center of Paris there are places just a stone's throw from Montmartre or the Champs Elysées which are well worth a visit, yet hardly known. The Marais quarter around the modern bulk of the Pompidou Center is full of beautiful old mansions, and has recently been restored to the glorious state it enjoyed during the reign of Henry IV. Turn a little corner by the Comédie Française and take a morning stroll through the gardens of the Palais Royal, or step only a short distance from the Louvre and the rue de Rivoli into the Marais to see the beautiful Place des Vosges. This was once a tournament ground, the place where the knight Montgomery, Captain of the Scottish guard, accidentally wounded Henri II, causing the king's death a few days later. In those days this was the Place des Combats, but in 1799 the government, desperate for money, announced that they would rename this beautiful square in honor of the first *département* to pay its taxes, and the Vosges won; it is hard to imagine such an offer working in any other country!

Such delightful corners abound in Paris and multiply endlessly as the traveler moves out into the countryside and deeper into the heartland of France. Visit Versailles, yes, but do not ignore the valley of Chevreuse; or go a little to the north and east and see the beautiful Château of Chantilly, once the home of the Princess of

Condé, which now contains a marvelous museum. Do not miss the great castle, or *château-fort,* at Provins to the east, or the fortified bridge and old houses at Moret-sur-Loing.

Even closer to Paris, a short bus ride from the center, stands Vincennes, an historic spot in a beautiful park, and visitors who go south to see the great palace of Fontainebleau should stop over in the forest which surrounds it, perhaps at Barbizon, a charming village and an artists' center, once very popular with the Impressionists. To get off the beaten track in France is not too difficult, even if done idly, but those who go to France determined to get below the surface of this diverse and beautiful country can do even better if they will take a little time and effort.

If pressed to suggest a part of France which is both beautiful and like nowhere else on earth I would point my enquirers towards the Auvergne, the green country of the Massif Central. Here the traveler can see the striking and marvelous country of the

Chaine des Puys, which lies west of Clermont-Ferrand, an area sprinkled with the round cones of long-extinct volcanoes. Travel on to the pilgrim city of Le Puy in the Vélay, the starting point for The Road to the Shrine of St James, a thousand miles away at Compostela in Spain, a marvelous road to follow across France. Le Puy itself has a vast cathedral and on one of those spikes of rock, or *puys,* which give the town its name is set the little Chapel of St Michel, a wonderful sight. The Auvergne today is a wild, half-populated country, full of those hidden corners which true travelers like to find.

Closer to Paris, a mere hundred miles away across the flat plain of the Beauce, and Normandy, lies Brittany, a popular province certainly, but one where the tourists gather in quantity only at Mont-Saint-Michel, St Malo, or Dinan, which are all worth seeing but not nearly enough for a true traveler. Go further west still, into Finistère, to the villages of St Thégonnec or Lampaul-Guimiliau, to see the best of the Breton

calvaries, or head south to 'the land of the little sea', the Morbihan, to the town of Vannes, still encircled by medieval walls, or see the little port of Auray where in 1776 Benjamin Franklin stepped ashore, the first ambassador from America to France.

Normandy was smashed to pieces in the fighting which followed the D-Day landings of 1944, but the old towns have been so well restored that you will hardly notice. This is farming country rich in cattle, cheese, cream and cider, but Rouen, where Joan of Arc was burned at the stake, is a fine city and a great port on the Seine. Spend a day in Rouen to wander about the old *quartier* by the cathedral, before setting off to the west through Caen, ancient capital of William the Conqueror, to Bayeux, where the celebrated tapestry which records the invasion of England in 1066 is housed in a fine new museum.

And so on to the beautiful Cotentin country of the Cherbourg peninsula. Americans were here in abundance in 1944, for these flat fields and low rolling hills were

Top left Centerpiece of Louis XIV's great palace, the Hall of Mirrors at Versailles, where the treaty was signed to end the Great War of 1914-1918.

Above The great hunting lodge of Fontainebleau was the favorite residence of French kings before the building of Versailles in the early eighteenth century.

Left A view of Place des Vosges, a wonderfully quiet square in Paris lined with arches and magnificent sixteenth-century houses.

Above The rich farming country of Normandy in the height of summer.

Right Formal gardens and old medieval houses set off the historic walls and turrets of the fortress city of Vannes in southern Brittany.

Far right A detail from the famous Bayeaux Tapestry shows the Normans setting sail for the conquest of England in 1066 and about to land at Pevensey.

the drop zones for the 101st and 82nd US Airborne. A worthwhile objective on a trip to the Cotentin would be a visit to the beautiful Parachute Museum set in Sainte-Mère-l'Église, south of Cherbourg.

Those who seek the sun while traveling in France are fairly sure to find it when they get anywhere south of the Loire, that long river which flows for six hundred miles from the Ardèche and runs into the Atlantic near St Nazaire. Any traveler heading south has to cross the Loire, and most choose to do so through the châteaux country of Touraine, which has such famous palaces as Chambord and, most beautiful of all, the Château Chenonceaux. To see a few of these great palaces of the Valois kings is always worthwhile, but hidden France hereabouts lies a little to the east. I should explain that while a *château* in France can be any large country house, a castle with drawbridge and battlement is a *château-fort,* and the finest of these are found in Anjou, the ancient homeland of the Plantagenet kings who ruled in England and much of France until 1485. The best of these castles lie at Saumur and Angers, and overlook the Seine.

From here, after visiting the Plantagenet mausoleum in the abbey at Fontevrault where Richard the Lionheart lies buried, we can follow the Plantagenets south across Poitou and the Limousin into the green river country of the Dordogne. This is Périgord, rich in food, wine and history, the food all cream and truffles, the wines of Bordeaux and St Emilion, the history from the jarring decades of the Hundred Years' War. Inevitably the Dordogne is popular with tourists, and no visitor should fail to visit little golden Domme, the castles at Beynac

or Montfort or, further to the east, the great caves of Padirac, or the fantastic little pilgrim town of Rocamadour, where the houses cling to the sheer sides of a gorge. Our task though, is to find those other, out-of-the-way places, so here we veer south, into the *bastide* country, to see the attractive little towns, each a relic of the Valois-Plantagenet wars, at Villeréal, Villefranche or Montpazier, all quite delightful. If we enjoy beauty and a touch of grandeur then the castle of Biron is a splendid pile, dating from the High Middle Ages, beautifully preserved and hardly ever visited.

This river country of France, which runs east from the Gironde to the foothills of the Auvergne, is full of such beautiful places. Before leaving, travelers should try to see the castle of Michel de Montaigne, ancient Libourne, and two more exquisite little towns, Bourdeilles and Brantôme, before turning south again for two great river valleys which lie a little off that well-trodden track, those of the Tarn and the Lot.

Here again there are popular places along the rivers, each well worth a visit, such as the Gorges of the Tarn, which the more intrepid travelers can descend by boat. Those who prefer the other, quieter

Right The slopes of the escarpment, north and south of the little Burgundian town of Beaune, are clocked with vines, producing the famous vintages of the Côtes de Nuit and the Côtes de Beaune.

Below An early morning view of Chenonceaux reflected in the waters of the Cher, built by Henri II of France for his beautiful mistress, the beguiling Diane de Poitiers.

13

Right Deep green valleys, small villages and forest-draped hillsides are typical of the wild, beautiful country of the Auvergne.

Below Perched on a sharp, rocky hill or 'puy' the little pilgrim church of St Michel l'Aiguihle in Le Puy, is one of several pillar churches dedicated to Saint Michael.

parts of France should go to Cahors, capital of the wine country of Quercy, to see the famous Pont Valentré before moving a little further south, on minor roads if possible, to the town of Moissac. Here the great Church of St Pierre has a fabled west door and richly carved cloisters, not to mention a splendid hotel nearby, the *Chapon-Fin.* Those who come this way, wandering down the river valleys from the Central Auvergne, will have had a marvelous journey down the Lot, through three wonderfully picturesque riverside towns, Estaing, Espalion and Entraygues. After this it is possible to climb over the mountains into the remote Rouergue, to see the little hill-town of Conques, which has a great pilgrim church, and treasure dating back to Charlemagne.

One can find such places all over France, in the Alps, in the green north country of the Vosges, even just behind the ever-popular Riviera, but to conclude this look at hidden France we can head south towards the distant loom of the Pyrénées, across the Armagnac country, the home of D'Artagnan and the Three Musketeers, to see elegant Pau, to the Lourdes of Ste Bernadette, into the dancing country of the Basques and the Catalans. In the Basque country, visit little St-Jean-Pied-de-Port at the foot of the pass of Roncevaux and some of the little Basque villages round about. Then turn east across the grain of these high southern mountains where as the green turns to gold the traveler climbs to the high plateau of the Cerdagne, a place surrounded even in summer by snow-tipped peaks, before sweeping down to the wine-drenched plain of Roussillon, home of the French Catalans, and into historic Perpignan. This is Roussillon, full of pretty places, like Collioure, a little fishing port where painters come to marvel at the sights and colors. Turn a little north along the coast and enter the Languedoc; see Pézanas, Béziers, St Pons or Montpellier, which is one of those elegant university towns. Finally go to medieval Aigues-Mortes in the delta of the Rhône and there just across the river lies the Riviera, the Côte d'Azur, crammed with visitors, but over here in the Languedoc we are still in a country that the tourists have yet to discover. Just go there soon, before they do.

Left Looming high above the winding Dordogne, mighty Beynac castle still glowers south across the valley.

Left Summer on the sand, anywhere along the great sweep of the *Baie des Anges,* between Nice and Cannes.

Below Seen across the harbor at Collioure, the rose-tipped roof of the old Roman *phare* or lighthouse overlooks the red roofs of the town.

An evening in the picturesque little Norman port of Honfleur, on the Bay of the Seine, a place full of yachts and the smell of the sea; a noted center for artists.

Towns and Cities

France is one of those fortunate countries with very few large cities and those that are there tend to be very different from each other, each a provincial capital in its own right. The real glory of urban France, however, lies more in the vast number of smaller towns which have developed to a sensible size. Where they have been rebuilt at all it has been done in a style which matches the surroundings and creates a pleasant whole.

This is a generality alas, not the invariable rule; it cannot be said that the modern towers and tenements of La Défense do much to challenge, let alone enhance, the glorious boulevards which remain from Haussman's Paris of the 1870s, but even in Paris there are places which no observant and appreciative visitor should miss. At present the old Halles are being redeveloped and the resulting changes have revealed the old church and squares near the Fontaine des Innocents, while the cleaning and restoring of the Marais *quartier* is a tribute to the good taste and wisdom of the municipality of Paris and an example for town councils everywhere.

Apart from Paris, France is full of splendid towns and cities. One of the best ways to see a fair selection of towns in a limited time is to take a tour around the cathedral cities, especially those in the north, where the great church in the center of the city is a poem in stone, a classic example of the soaring verticality of the Gothic. The Gothic style owes its beginning to the genius of Archbishop Suger, who began his work at St Denis on the northern outskirts of Paris, but it reached its peak, or so the experts say, at Chartres.

Chartres is best seen twice on the first visit, which is not difficult for those who approach this city across the flat grainfields of the Beauce. From there one first sees the cathedral rising above the city like a great stone ship, a breathtaking sight. Then wait until you stand in the square before the west door under the soaring pinnacles, or until you are inside in the vast, gloomy interior, preferably at a time when the bells are clamoring above or the organ thunders out for the evening service – that's how to feel the glory of the Gothic and catch a little of that spirit which inspired those medieval craftsmen who built these marvelous churches.

A tour of these great cathedrals should include Rouen, which like a number of French churches has a Butter Tower built from money paid by those who preferred not to give up rich food during Lent; Amiens, a solid building that still sits delicately in the center of the town; and Rheims, which is still evocative of that day when Joan of Arc led her *'gentil dauphin'* here to his coronation, dominating the city as it has for centuries.

One must avoid any tour of France becoming a progress in and out of church doors, inducing culture glut. Besides, in a country of such variety there is no need to limit oneself. To the east lies Strasbourg, a very fine provincial city, full of canals and notably good restaurants, and in the southern half of the country lie two others almost equally splendid: Besançon, still overtopped by Vauban's great fortress, and almost in the center of France the beautiful city of Lyon. Lyon stands on the junction of the Rhône and Saône rivers, and is noted as being the gastronomic capital of France, full of good restaurants, good nightlife and, best of all, good wine.

Follow the Rhône south and you will come to Marseilles, a great seaport, and in spite of the ravages of the Second World War still an attractive city, as is Toulouse, the red-stone capital of the old Languedoc, the country of Cathars and troubadours. Toulouse has the great cathedral of St Sernin and a marvelous central square, the Place du Capitole, and is well worth a stop before following the Garonne river north to Bordeaux, a rather English city. This is not surprising since the English possessed Bordeaux from 1140 to 1452, a period which some of the present inhabitants still look back on as a golden age.

France is full of such cities and to those listed above we could add Perpignan, the

Above The kings of France were crowned in the cathedral at Rheims for nearly a thousand years, and it remains a magnificent, regal building.

Right Orléans, set on the broad sweep of the Loire is a pleasant provincial city, the place where Joan of Arc defeated the English in 1429.

Far right Stained glass, filtering the sunlight, casts multicolored light into the great vault of Chartres Cathedral.

capital of French Catalonia; Dijon, the capital of Burgundy; Nancy, Orléans, Caen, Limoges, to name only a few – so, let us leave the great cities of France and look instead at some of the smaller towns.

Beaune is very small, with a resident population of only 20000, but is a capital in its own right, of the wine country of Burgundy. The hills of the Côtes de Nuits and the Côtes de Beaune lie north and south of the old walls, while as a central gem the town contains the medieval hospital the Hôtel-Dieu, built in the fifteenth century from the revenues of the wine trade by Nicolas Rolin, Chancellor to Philip the Good, Duke of Burgundy. Burgundy is full of little towns like Beaune, each a medieval masterpiece, so those who have the time should also visit Vézelay, Nolay, Noyers, Chablis, Auxerre – even in this single province the visitor is glutted with choice.

The same is true of almost every part of France, so that travelers in the Ile de France, the region round Paris, would be well advised to add Rambouillet, Beauvais and Compiègne to their list of major places, and spare some time for two lesser-known delights, at Crépy-en-Valois to the east, and medieval Gisors in the Vexin, which lies on the border with Normandy.

Normandy and Brittany cannot really be appreciated by visitors who have never seen Honfleur, Bayeux and William the Conqueror's birthplace at Falaise. In Brittany take a day each to see St Malo, Dinan, Vannes, and travel down the eastern frontier to the cities of Vitré and Fougères, a necessary part of any in-depth tour of these two delightful and very different provinces.

The Val de Loire is one of those ever-popular places which are, well, ever-popular, but it is still nice to visit a few places which lie off the coach-and-car-crammed tourist routes. Blois is a very fine city, the virtual capital of France during the last days of the Valois kings and the castle of Amboise is not notably less splendid than the better-known châteaux round about. Turn south-east at Blois and follow the river upstream to yet another cathedral city, Bourges. This was also in its day the seat of the French Court, at a time when the English were enjoying their last years of glory before Joan of Arc rode to raise the siege of Orléans in 1429 and drove them out of France for ever. South of Bourges lies the Bourbonnais, a region full of fine towns and cities; Nevers, Moulins, Châteauroux and, another little gem, Paray-le-Monial, all meriting a visit.

Between central France and the Pyrénées the traveler can wander at will and never lack an attractive town or city in which to spend the night, or add pleasure to

Far left Poppies by the roadside set off a view across the green and gold country of Normandy.

Left The view across the valley from the ramparts of the castle at Najac in the Auvergne, one of the greatest castles of southern France.

Below Provence, the *provincia romana* still retains many great relics of the Roman Empire as illustrated here, where a bust of Augustus Caesar overlooks an entrance to the amphitheater.

the passing day. See Albi, which has a vast red cathedral and a museum crammed with works by Toulouse-Lautrec, who was born here. See Cahors, if only for the bridge, and Moissac, if only for the tympanum over the church door. Visit Auch in the Armagnac country, or Montauban, or Aurillac in the Rouergue, each the archetype of a French town, each a place with comfortable hotels, narrow streets, good inexpensive restaurants and, if you are lucky, a merciful absence of tourists.

The hinterlands of France provide attractions for differing tastes and preferences. Those who relish a flavor of the past, for example, will enjoy a trip across France that will take in most of the best medieval cities. Here one might start at Provins, east of Paris, still overlooked by a great fortress tower, and cut south to Melun and historic Orléans. Turn downstream to little Beaugency, once fortified against the English by Dunois, Joan of Arc's great captain, before traveling on to Chinon, a splendid spot where a castle crowns the bridge above the river. South of Chinon lies Loudun, once the home of Cardinal Richelieu, and from here it is a short day's journey to the Dordogne country, to Sarlat, a medieval gem, and on across Quercy to little Martel and the town of Rocamadour. From here see Cahors, then turn up the Lot to Estaing and Conques, before cutting south towards two of the great cities of medieval France, Carcassonne and Aigues-Mortes, which still look very much as they did five hundred years ago. Carcassonne is, alas, a tourist trap, a place best visited out of season, but Aigues-Mortes is actually smaller today than it was when St Louis used it as the port for his Crusades, and has shrunk back within its medieval walls.

France caters for the lovers of many other epochs besides the Middle Ages. For a contrast those who seek the cheerful, lively

Right Cobbled streets lead into the center of Dinan, one of the finest medieval towns in Brittany, and essential stop for visitors touring the north coast of the province.

Below left Strasbourg, now the home of the European Parliament, is a fine city, the commercial center for the province of Alsace-Lorraine.

world of the twentieth-century traveler will find plenty of choice there too. The entire French coast along the Mediterranean is crowded with attractive resorts, each full of bars and discos, nightclubs, restaurants and everything one could want for a high old time. Try Collioure, Sète, Montpellier, La Grande Motte, classic Monte Carlo, Cannes or Nice. Try the university cities, Toulouse or Lyon, always lively in the student *quartier;* wander the west coast, from Biarritz to Arcachon, or take care to arrive in some small wine-drenched center in time to share the festivities which always follow the gathering of that year's vintage – at the wine festival of Béziers, held every August 15, the wine literally flows from the fountains in the town square.

Finally, there in the north lies the *ville lumière,* Paris, the city of light, that embracing capital with a vibrant lifestyle that never stops and reaches from Pigalle to the Boulevard St Michel, and lies in wait in cellars and cafés and nightclubs. This is a city for all seasons, a magnet for France and the world.

Left Rich carvings adorn the fine Renaissance buildings in Blois, where the Valois Kings of France maintained their court.

Right Red roofs, rocky hillsides, a hint of lavender in the air and not too far away, the sea. This typical view of Provence is at Aiguines.

Below .The waters of the Lot reflect the towers of the castle of Estaing, which dates back to the thirteenth century and defends the bridge across the river.

Far left Market day in Sarlat, one of the lovely old towns found in the Dordogne.

Left Soiree de Paris! And where better to spend an evening watching a show than at the Paradis Latin.

Below Set in the center of Monte Carlo, the Hôtel de Paris has been a fashionable hotel since the early days of the present century, and still draws in the crowds.

Seen from across the vineyard, the walls and towers of Carcassonne have defied armies for nearly a thousand years and illustrate the full magnificence of a medieval fortress.

A great sweep of blue sea, a host of umbrellas laid out along the beach, all basking in the sun — that's the daily scene on the Riviera coast of France.

Beautiful Beaches

France has three very different coastlines offering beautiful beaches: the Atlantic Ocean, the Mediterranean Sea and the English Channel or, as the French prefer to call it, *La Manche*. This all adds up to a vast quantity of seacoast, and a wide variety of beach, from the sandy coves of Brittany to the surfer's paradise of Biarritz, or those sun-worshippers' topless havens which reach along the Riviera from St Tropez to Menton. Take beaches as the common link and they provide the perfect theme for a varied tour of the coast of France, which can begin on the Channel coast opposite the famous white cliffs of Dover, on the flat beaches by Cap Griz-Nez where high-speed hovercraft and cross-Channel swimmers sweep or crawl ashore. These are wide, sandy beaches, fringed today with windsurfers, and the coast becomes fashionable just a little to the south at Le Touquet, which is one of the weekend playgrounds for *Tout Paris,* the high society of the capital, just an hour or two away by car or train.

Dieppe also has a ferry port, and a beach of shingle and stones, but those who move south along the coastal cliffs above the bay of the Seine will find a host of little coves and bays, each with its port and *plage*. There is Yport, and Fécamp, and Étretat, this last with a beach overlooked by chalk cliffs carved into fantastic shapes by the constant action of the Channel seas.

Across the Bay of the Seine lies little Honfleur, a real gem, and then the Normandy beaches begin, those strands of fatal memory, the *plages des débarquement,* the landing beaches of 1944, Gold, Juno, Sword, Utah, and between Arromanches and Grandcamp, bloody Omaha. Today they call this 40 mile stretch of sand the Côte de Nacre, the Pearl Coast, and apart from the memorials and the shattered casements of the Atlantic Wall there are few reminders of D-Day, but plenty to interest the veteran visitor, with museums at Bayeux and Arromanches and the vast American cemetery at St Laurent.

West of here, a buffer against the full force of the Atlantic gales, lies the Cherbourg peninsula. On the eastern side lies Utah Beach, flat and open, running up to a series of yachting centers and little ports like Barfleur and St Vaast before turning across Cherbourg into the little finger of land of the Cap de la Hague, from where the British Channel Island of Alderney is almost within touching distance. This western shore of the peninsula is high and rocky, but there are good beaches here too, notably at Portbail and Barneville Carteret. Further south, beyond Granville, they say it is possible to walk across the sands to Mont-St-Michel when the tide is out, but those who attempt this trip will need a guide, for the tide sweeps back swiftly, and the distance across is much further than it looks.

Brittany has a long jagged coastline, full of headlands, bays and beaches, but along this northern shore there are few places to compare with Sables-d'Or-les-Pins, or Erquy on the Côte d'Emeraude or further west, the beaches near Paimpol, Perros-Guirec or Trégastel on the Côte de Granit Rose, the Granite Rose Coast, where the rocks are pink and make the perfect contrast to the golden sand and the clear, blue sea.

Turn south across the headlands of Finistère and you will find long beaches and little ports everywhere, at Douarnenez, around Morgat and Camaret in the peninsula of Crozon, or around Audierne. Brittany is justly famous for its beaches and they are so plentiful that they never really get crowded. The exceptions to this sweeping statement would be along the Quiberon peninsula, where sand-yachting is popular and, of course, at the popular and fashionable resort of La Baule, an elegant Edwardian resort where great hotels line the promenade behind a long beach crammed with sunbathers and dotted with little cafés, each with a colorful burst of parasols set against the scorching summer sun.

If Brittany is famous for its beaches, then the country to the south deserves to be. This is the Vendée, one of those areas where most of the summer visitors are French, a place which visitors from other countries have yet to discover. This whole western coast from the Loire to the Gironde is a series of long, beautiful beaches, each backed with an attractive town or a string of

Far left The waves and currents of the Channel have carved the chalk cliffs of Etretat into these wonderful shapes.

Left Erquay, a fishing port of the Côtes-du-Nord in Brittany, full of offshore trawlers.

Below Great medieval towers guard the entrance to the old port of La Rochelle, once a Huguenot stronghold, now a fishing port and yachting center for the Vendée.

Below A balmy day on the beach of Biarritz, a paradise for sun lovers and surfers.

Right The clear, warm waters of the rocky coast of Corsica are alive in summer with boardsailers and yachtsmen.

small, picturesque villages, while offshore lie some islands that every traveler should visit. One can begin at Noirmoutier, an offshore paradise, and travel on to the pretty resort of Pornic on the mainland, before cutting south for a trip to the little Ile d'Yeu, and the great long sweep of Les Sables d'Olonne – and look for that word *sables,* which means 'sand' and is usually the sign of a good beach. South of Les Sables d'Olonne lie still more attractive offshore islands, the Ile de Ré and the Ile d'Oleron, while no traveler, however devoted to sunbathing he or she may be, should pass this way without a visit to the little port of Rochefort, or the historic town of La Rochelle.

Beyond the great estuary of the Gironde lies the flat pine-tree country of the Landes. This part of the Atlantic coast is being

developed into a resort area, and is already studded with little villages and has one large modern complex, the town of Arcachon. Arcachon is mostly modern, but it lies around an old fishing port, and overlooks an attractive sheltered bay, ideal for all kinds of water sports, sailing, windsurfing, scuba diving, fishing, water-skiing. In these warm waters the sea is a constant source of pleasure and delight.

South of Arcachon lies the Côte d'Argent, the Silver Coast, a 170-mile sweep of sand facing out into the Bay of Biscay and the Atlantic. Here the great waves come thundering in, to make surfing the great sport, especially with the sun-and-salt-bleached young who gather here in great numbers during the summer. Those who prefer somewhere or something more restful and elegant will not be disappointed in Biarritz.

Biarritz has slipped a little from the modern mind, but at the turn of the century and between the wars it was the resort for the kings, nobility and glitterrati of European society, owning much of its fame to such notables as Edward VII of England, and the Empress Eugénie of France. Biarritz retains a certain splendor from those gracious days, with majestic hotels, excellent restaurants, an elegant promenade where noble lords once doffed their top-hats to ladies of doubtful virtue, and it still has, above all, a distinct air of style. A little to the south lie two smaller resorts well worth a look at St Jean-de-Luz and Hendaye, but here we must leave the

Atlantic and skip across the Pyrénées to the softer, warmer shores and seas of the Mediterranean.

The Mediterranean coast of France, which runs from the frontier with Spain to the frontier with Italy, can be divided into two fairly equal regions, split by the delta of the Rhône, which flows into the sea by the marshlands of the Camargue. To the north-east of this wildlife sanctuary lies the Riviera, to the south and west the long beaches of Languedoc and Roussillon.

The coasts of Roussillon begin with some little fishing ports, with shingle beaches but nevertheless attractive in spite of the stones. There are few places to match Collioure or Banyuls, and anyway, the sand begins again at Argelès and runs without interruption around the Gulf of Lions to the Rhône and beyond. Like the coastline of the Landes, this region has been developed as a resort area, and is now well supplied with holiday centers, each with a yachting marina, hotels, apartment blocks, cafés, discos and, of course, beaches. Some of these are nudist beaches and one resort, Cap d'Agde, has a part of the town

completely devoted to nudism, while going topless is accepted everywhere. Some of these resorts, like Port Barcarès, Port Leucate and above all, La Grande Motte, are built in the most futuristic architectural styles, but somehow they look attractive, blessed as they are with clear skies for a backdrop and the summer sun to set them off. Those who like somewhere a little less stark to stay in after a day on the beach will find their ideal choice among such places as Narbonne, Valras Plage, Le Grau du Roi, or Sète, a port which is the Mediterranean terminus for that beautiful waterway, the Canal du Midi, which curves in to the sea here after wandering across the Midi from Toulouse.

This long, long, Languedoc beach, over 140 miles of it, is backed behind the coast by a long string of shallow, salt-water lakes or *étangs*. These are used to grow seafood, mussels, oysters, shrimps and lobsters, and provide a feeding ground for hundreds of pink flamingoes which breed in the Camargue. Needless to add that watersports are available everywhere, and those who enjoy a little history and culture

Bottom left Morning in the crowded harbor of Vieux Port, fishermen prepare their nets before shipping out to sea.

Left The coastline of L'Esterel, west of Nice, wild and desolate, is a refreshing contrast to the crowded beaches on the nearby Côte d'Azur.

Below A view of the pyramids and ziggurats of La Grande Motte, one of the modern resorts on the Languedoc coast of France, south of Montpellier.

can break away from this golden coast to visit Béziers, Pézenas, Montpellier, Nîmes or the Crusader port of Aigues-Mortes.

Across the Rhône past Marseille the Côte d'Azur begins. This is the Riviera, a place newly discovered as a summer playground, for in the 1920s and 30s when the area was more fashionable and less popular than it is today, no one who was anyone would have dreamed of visiting the Riviera in summer; from April to October the Riviera was dead!

Well, all that has changed and a lot more besides. Here, today, hedonism rules. It begins just east of Marseille, among the *calanques,* little bays and beaches hidden in the indented coastline which runs towards Bandol. Good places here are La Ciotat, Cassis, and above all, Sanary, a little string of resorts a lot quieter than the more popular places to the east. Offshore lie the Iles d'Hyères, and then beyond Le Lavandou, the modern Riviera begins, Port Grimaud, St Tropez, Ste Maxime, St Aygulf, places crammed in summer with the young and fashionable, or the not-so-young and not-so-fashionable, all hoping to mix and mingle. More truly *au-fait* are Cannes and Nice, or a handful of little towns which lie behind the coast, Vence, Cagnes, and St-Paul-de-Vence, which are less crowded and more ancient than such well-known resorts as Antibes or Juan-les-Pins. All are worth a look before we travel along the *Corniche,* past Cap Ferrat, to skirt the principality of Monaco, or take a look at Monte Carlo and finish our tour around the coastline of France with a touch of old world charm on the promenade at Menton. If time permits we can take a ferry boat south for 50 miles to the romantic island of Corsica, another place where beaches and rocky coves alternate around a coastline noted for its beauty.

Traveling like this around the coast of France will take the visitor a long way, but via a host of different places, all of them interesting. Many, indeed, will rank among the most beautiful places on earth, and all merit a visit.

Far left A sweep of sea and sharp rocky headlands enclose some of the smaller beaches at the western end of the Côte d'Azur.

Left above The bright, contrasting colors of craft and nets turn this work-a-day scene in Corsica into a memorable picture.

Left below A night view of the harbor at Monte Carlo.

41

Summer in Savoie, in the green mountains south of Lake Geneva, a skier's paradise in winter.

CHAPTER 4

Lakes, Mountains and Rivers

Mention the word France to your friends and you can see the image it conjures up in their minds: Paris, wine, beaches, casinos, but rarely unless they think of skiing, the lakes, rivers and mountains which so beautify the landscape of France. And yet France is really a rural country with a handful of great cities, where most of the industry is concentrated in the north or on the outskirts of the provincial capitals. For the most part France is a land of countryside.

There are three distinct mountain ranges in the Alps, the Pyréneés and the Massif Central, plus a host of smaller but no less attractive hills, the Cevennes, the Jura and the Corbières, to name but a few. Think of rivers: where can one match for beauty the valleys of the Loire, the Tarn, the Lot or the rushing streams of the Pyrénées? Here and there you find the ever-lovely lake country, in the *départements* of the Doubs and Jura or the Ain, north and east of Lyon. Think of France then, and think of its natural attractions, in river, lake and mountain, more varied in size, form and beauty here than anywhere else in Europe.

Take lakes: France does not have anything to match for size the Great Lakes of North America, but when it comes to beauty, she can compete with anywhere. Perhaps the finest lakes of France are those of the Jura, tucked into the line of low, rolling hills which march along the Swiss frontier, or lie further south, spattered across the green canvas of the Ain and the Bugey, north-east of Lyon, where one memorable lake sets off to perfection the little resort town of Nantua. In Burgundy most of the lakes are in fact reservoirs, but they are none the less lovely for that, especially those set, like Les Settons, in the great wilderness park of the Morvan. Further south those who travel to the sun on minor roads can leave Rodez, the red capital of the Aveyron, and come shortly to the vast lake of Pareloup, south of Pont de Salars, which is practically an inland sea. This great lake is fringed, as it should be, with beaches, camp sites and small villages, the perfect place in which to linger on a trip to the crowded coast of the Mediterranean.

As for mountains, France can claim the cream of the European peaks, or at worst, share them reluctantly with her neighbors. The French may call it Mont Blanc, the Italians Monte Bianco, but either way it is the highest peak in Western Europe at 15 770 feet (4807 meters).

The French Alps may be said to begin on the shores of Lac Léman (or Lake Geneva), and from here they march south for over two hundred miles to plunge, at last, into the Mediterranean. From the north they offer first the country of Haute Savoie, a great skiing area, full of resorts, many with those interlinked lift systems which create such vast ski areas as the Portes du Soleil, around Champéry and Avoriaz, or the Trois Vallées, between Courcheval and Val

Thorens. These are post-Second World War resorts, built high in the mountains, well above the snowline, but their names are already famous among winter sports enthusiasts; Avoriaz, Les Gets, Méribel, La Plagne, places fit to rank with Megève or Chamonix, Les Deux Alpes or Alpe d'Huez, which grew as the sport of skiing developed in the 1930s and 1940s.

Skiing is a fairly modern eruption in these mountains, however, and in a bid to preserve the best of their natural heritage, the French Alps are now dotted with a number of national parks, where industry is banned and commerce discouraged. The Parc de la Vanoise overhangs Val d'Isère, while below the great peak of Le Meije by Les Deux-Alpes, the rugged Parc des Ecrins, a region noted for glaciers, spreads across the country to Briançon and the neighboring Parc of Queyras, which runs along the Italian frontier. Further south in the Alpes Maritimes lies the newest of these national parks, the Parc du Mercantour,

Right Lac Sautet, a blue, beach-fringed lake.

Below Le Salagou is a man-made lake.

where the prehistoric carvings in the remote Vallée des Merveilles attract visitors from all over the world.

These Alps however, contain only the main peaks; from here great spurs run off into the countryside, and each far-flung outcrop provides its own, very different aspect to the countryside of France. South of Grenoble, for example, lies the high plateau of the Vercors, while as a backdrop to the Riviera a whole range of hills run behind the coast, each a little, rarely-visited paradise. Who can remember visiting the Massif des Maures, or the wine country of the Luberon? Yet there they are, in easy sight and reach, just a few miles inland from the bikini-crammed beaches of the Côte d'Azur.

In Central France, in the old country of the Auvergne, lie the hills of the Massif Central, remote, somewhat desolate, increasingly depopulated, snow-capped in winter, a paradise for walkers in summer. They climb steadily to 6000 feet (18000 meters), at the Plomb du Cantal, and give great views to west and east from the heights of Mont-Dore, south of Clermont-Ferrand. This is a region of high hills, steep-sided valleys, little winding roads, small country hotels and is quite delightful. If all this is still not enough,

Left France can lay claim to the largest skiing areas in the world.

Bottom left The Alps are well provided with cable car systems or mountain railways, a perfect way to see the sights, as here above Chamonix.

Below Looking down on to a steep snowcovered Alpine hillside where generations of toil have produced this small village with terraced fields for crops.

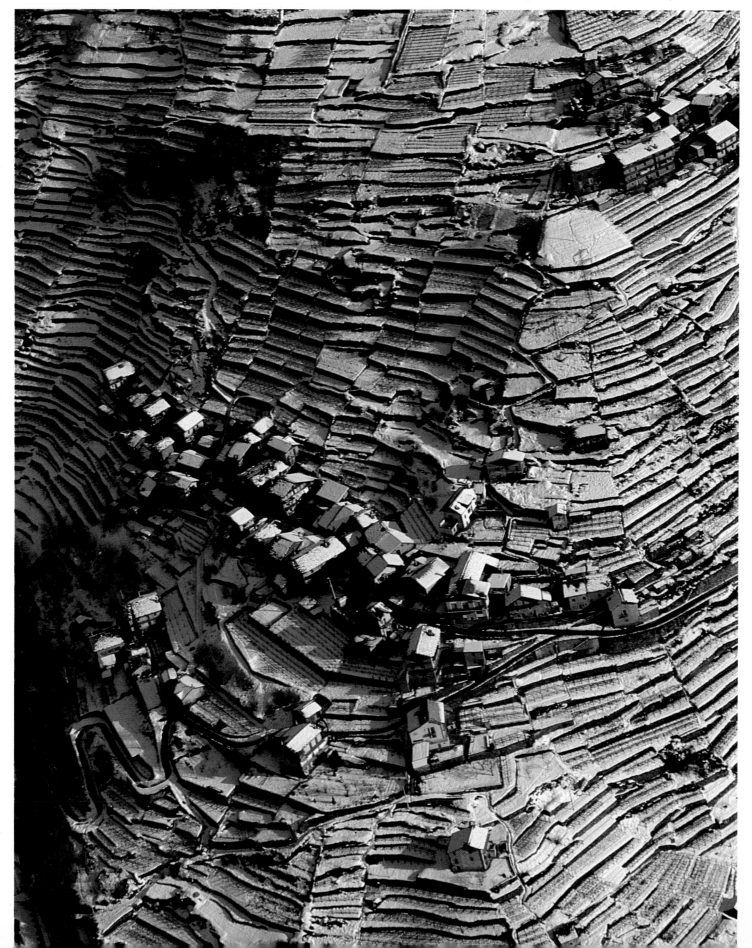

then a little to the south and east lie the Cévennes, a place made famous by the Scots writer Robert Louis Stevenson over a hundred years ago, when he wandered over these hills accompanied only by '…a small grey donkey called Modestine, the colour of a mouse, and with a kindly eye'. The story of their journey, *Travels with a Donkey in the Cévennes,* is still considered one of the world's great travel books, but the Cévennes remain much as they were when Stevenson passed this way, remote, sunscorched, and very beautiful.

Look at any topographic map of France and you will find such rare hill country almost everywhere, and everyone who knows France well will have a favorite place to wander in, be it the Vosges of the north,

that green tongue of country between the old provinces of Alsace and Lorraine, or the little-visited country of the Espinouse, which lies far to the east of Toulouse. With a choice like this one can afford to be subjective so, while admitting to a passion for the Auvergne and a fondness for the Cévennes, it seems fair to draw the reader's attention to the mountains and foothills of the French Pyrénées, my favorite out-of-the-way part of France.

The Pyrénées span the land between the Atlantic and the Mediterranean, and mark the frontier with Spain. Whereas the southern slopes run far out into the plains of Aragon and Catalonia, the French slopes are much steeper and more dramatic. They can be seen at their best from a certain

small road, the Route des Cols, which runs for over 250 miles across these bare mountains, in and out of the deep valleys, climbing round corkscrew bends to one windy pass (or *col*), before descending breathlessly into another valley, and then up again to the top; not a route for the nervous or those in a hurry, with great voids yawning out beside the road.

This road begins at Bayonne and, after heading east to St Jean-Pied-de-Port, climbs over the Col d'Osquich (a baby peak at only 1500 feet), getting into its stride among the Haute Pyrénées, past Tardets and Aramits, up to Arette, over the Col d'Aubisque, east of Gourette, down to Luz St Sauveur and Cauterets in the Parc des Pyrénées, and so on, up and down over

Left The ridge of the Massif Central is seen in this picture of Le Puy Marie.

Below, left Snow-capped even in the hottest days of the long French summer, the 15 770 ft peak of Mont Blanc, Europe's highest mountain, overlooks the valley of Chamonix.

Below, right The Pyrénées village of St Jean Pied de Port; although lower than the Alps, the Pyrénées are no less beautiful.

these glorious windy hills, eventually down to the sea at Banyuls. On the way the traveler will pass all the great peaks and valleys of the Pyrénées, the Pic du Midi d'Ossau, the Val d'Aran, and Mont Canigou, the last the great mountain of the Catalans. If all this is too steep and airy there are other, smaller foothills nearby, the Aspères, the Corbières, the Fénouillades, all remote, each glorious in its own special way.

Finally, what of those rivers which have done so much to shape the world's conception of France? The Seine does not just flow briefly through Paris, and the Loire devotes only a little of its time to enhancing the hunting lodges and palaces of the châteaux country. France is full of beautiful rivers, almost all deserving exploration. Of these, the Loire is the longest at 600 miles and arguably the most beautiful. It rises in the remote Ardèche as a mere trickle from the side of the Gerbier de Jonc, and reaches Le Puy before it comes to anything like full size. This is a river to follow west to the sea, past Nevers, into Touraine, the garden of France, and then Anjou, marking on its way the southern frontier of Brittany. The Garonne, that other famous river which bathes the vineyards of Bordeaux, rises in Spain and is still the Garona as it flows through Val d'Aran into France, while the Seine comes only a short distance from Burgundy on its journey to Paris and needs the assistance of the River Yonne to become that glinting night-time river that lovers love and singers sing about; once past Paris it becomes more imposing and beyond Rouen it is tidal and carries ocean-going ships all the way upstream to port.

Facing page Evening in Paris, looking down the stepladder bridges across the Seine.

Above Lyon, the second largest city in France sits on the banks of the Rhone.

Left The Loire, at 600 miles the longest river in France, is never lovelier than in the châteaux country, seen here from the walls of the castle at Saumur.

Go south and you will find a clutch of rivers which will make a theme for any journey. The Dordogne curves into the Garonne and forms the Gironde estuary after a delightful journey from the Massif Central. The Lot begins life as the Olt in the foothills of the Massif Central, and like the River Tarn is famous in France for the beauty of its deep, steep-sided gorges. To get a little away from these justly famous but rather over-popular streams, two final suggestions: follow the winding Aveyron through Najac and Penne and St Antonin-Nobel-Val, each rating a stop, or for somewhere almost savage in aspect go south to the town of Castellane in Provence, and from there plunge into the deep, dark depths of the Canyons de Verdon, where only the more daring climbers will attempt to scale the walls, and only well-equipped walkers are able to accomplish the two-day walk from one end of the Canyon to the other. Truly, France is a country with an almost limitless variety of natural attractions, and her lakes, rivers and hills are only a way into those parts of the country which other, more conventional travelers are rarely able to experience.

Below Pont d'Arc, a natural stone bridge over the Ardeche River.

Left Great rivers shape the steep valleys of the remote and beautiful Ardeche country, south of Lyon.

Below Set in the rugged country of Provence, the deep, sheer walls of the canyon of the Verdon river are a magnet for skilled rock climbers, and an awe-inspiring sight for less adventurous travelers.

Right There is at least half a *pont* at Avignon, all that remains of a pilgrim bridge built across the Rhone by an order of bridge building priests, the *Freres Pontiff,* in the thirteenth century.

Far right Erected in the fourteenth century with the supernatural assistance of the Devil, the mighty arches of the Pont Valentre still span the River Lot at Cahors.

Below The hills and rivers of the Herault *departement* in Languedoc combine to make many great swimming spots, like here in Cevenne.

Making good wine calls for ceaseless work, all year round. Here the grapes are being prepared for pressing.

Food and Drink

Nothing has done so much to attract visitors to France, or spread French culture about the world, as the national passion and excellence in the sphere of food and drink. This is something the French are not entirely happy about: they will refer the visitor's attention to France's achievements in literature and the arts, should he or she become too lyrical about the pleasure of the table, but whatever their doubts on the matter, in the world of *haute cuisine* France reigns supreme.

As to why this should be, there are probably three reasons. Firstly, France is by no means a homogenous country. It took a long time to grow to its present size, and in the process has absorbed a great many peoples, cultures – and cuisines. Travel about France and you will find dishes which owe their origin to Italy, Spain, Scandinavia, even England, and regional dishes peculiar to Normandy, Périgord, Catalonia or the Basque country. Secondly, France is blessed with rich land and a varied climate, which provides good fresh produce for the table. Lastly, and the most important of all, the French really care about food. The customers demand a high standard, and the restaurateurs either rise to meet it or go out of business.

Having said that, it is only fair to add that here, as elsewhere in the world, things are not as they once were. Prices have risen and the average standard has declined, most notably in the popular tourist centers. To eat well at a reasonable price in France it is necessary to look around, to pay attention to the better restaurant guides, and to avoid those places which get away with serving highly-priced but often mediocre food to less-than-discerning visitors.

However, France remains a country where one can often eat marvelously well, at very bearable prices, and as for the wine, what a choice! Apart from the great vintages of Bordeaux and Burgundy, there are marvelous local wines in almost every region, where the quality and choice improves year by year. There are wines from the Rhône and the Loire, from the Côtes de Roussillon, from Gaillac, from Arbois, from Brittany and the hills behind the Côte d'Azur, local wines which at their best complement the local food. Above all, there is champagne, a wine that goes with everything.

One of the curious things about wine and liqueur is the close affinity it occasionally has with the religious orders. Benedictine and Chartreuse are still produced by monks, while that sparkling champagne, the queen of wine, owes its very existence to a priest, Dom Pérignon. The center for champagne in France is the little town of Epernay, close to the city of Rheims, although most of the *vignerons* are based in the city nearby and store their wine in long, dark cellars which run for miles beneath the streets. In Rheims and Epernay the wine producers welcome visitors to inspect their cellars, sample the champagne, and of course, buy a bottle or a case to take home. Their example is followed in all the wine-growing areas of France, and one sign that you are entering a wine region is the growing number of *dégustation* or tasting stations set beside the road.

The two major wine-producing regions of France are Burgundy and Bordeaux. In Burgundy, Beaune is the center for the wine trade, the place where the wine is auctioned every November, and nearby at Clos Vougeot, the *Confrérie des Chevaliers du Tastevin* keeps watch on the high quality of the local wine. The *Chevaliers* were founded in 1933, and to be elected to their ranks is a great honor. Here again, other wine-growing areas have established similar bodies, all sharing a common interest in the production of the finest wine.

In Burgundy the traveler seems to be passing through a wine merchant's catalogue, through villages called Nuits-St-Georges, Chablis, Aloxe-Corton and Montrachet. Montrachet comes in various guises, as Chassagne-Montrachet or Puligny-Montrachet, but the supreme Montrachet, *Le Montrachet,* comes from one small, twenty-acre patch within a wall, which still manages to produce one of the finest white wines in the world.

The other great region for classic wines lies to the west, south of Bordeaux. This is the claret country, so called because of the clear *clarait* tint in the reds, as opposed to the slightly heavier reds of Burgundy. Bordeaux wines come from various chateaux, although many of them

Facing page, The vintage comes in the fall, somewhere between September and the end of October, in the various wine regions of France, and everyone joins in to gather the grapes.

Left True connoisseurs taste their wine from this little silver dish, called a *tastevin.* Different wines are sipped from different parts of the dish.

Below These deep caves which tunnel everywhere under the streets of Rheims and Epernay contain a liquid treasure of champagne.

PAIN DE CAMPAGNE CUIT AU BOIS

1.000 GRS

resemble nothing more imposing than farmhouses, but it is the wine that counts, and in a good year the wines of Bordeaux are excellent, and if left to mature and mellow, very valuable.

Great regions, good years and famous vintages apart, the traveler in France will find excellent, drinkable wine almost everywhere, wine which goes well with the local food and costs very little. In Brittany and the Western Loire Muscadet is the wine of the country and, well-chilled, goes wonderfully with the oysters and shellfish of the Atlantic coast, or the tender trout of the rivers. Around Lyon, that gastronomic heart of France, good wine abounds in the Beaujolais, at Fleurie, Morgon, and a score of other places, where they produce much more wine than the annual beaujolais nouveau and, incidentally, like to drink their red wine well-chilled, which can disconcert those people who are accustomed to red wine at room temperature.

Further south lie the vineyards of the Côtes du Rhône, of Châteauneuf du Pape and Hermitage, but these two are almost classic growths, and there are many other regional wines, no less delicious for being little known outside their local district. A good, chilled Perle from Gaillac on the Lot is delicious on a hot day, and no visitor dare linger by the old Pont Valentre without trying a bottle of the Bon Cahors, the black wine of Quercy. Those who like something lighter can try the wines of the Corbières or the Côtes de Roussillon or, around the mouth of the Rhône, a well-chilled, dry rosé, the Listel gris-de-gris.

And so it goes, all over France, wine for every taste and pocket, wine to complement every meal, and if the choice is vast, on one will go very far wrong in choosing the house wine, *le vin du patron.*

Food and wine are inseparable, as the French are prone to remark, 'A meal without wine is like a day without sunshine'. To find a good meal you must first find a good restaurant. To do this wise travelers consult their 'red' *Michelin* to find the local restaurants with a rosette or two, or turn to the *Guide Gault Millau,* where the ambience gets a rating as well as the food. If money is tight there are other rules. The restaurants recommended by the *Relais Routiers,* an organization of truck-drivers, are always worth inspecting, as are the hotel restaurants belonging to the *Logies de France,* all of which are privately owned and serve regional dishes. One might avoid them in other countries, but railway buffet restaurants are frequently good in France, and the one at the Gare du Nord in Paris is even famous. No one could really eat two full French meals in a day, so here again, wise travelers shop locally in the market for bread and wine, fruit and cheese, and have a picnic in the middle of the day. Every French town and most villages play host to a weekly market, where local produce is brought in from the surrounding countryside. Here the visitor will find French produce at its finest: home-cooked patés, sausages, fresh farm eggs, an immense variety of cheeses, (General de Gaulle bewailed the difficulty of governing a country that produced over three hundred different kinds of cheese), fresh bread, delicious gateaux, and that wealth of fruit and vegetables which provide the basis for the marvelous cooking which everyone here enjoys and appreciates.

In recent years a reluctance to tackle the full, rich glories of French cuisine has led to the introduction of a new, lighter style of cooking, *cuisine nouvelle,* which avoids heavy sauces and richer ingredients in favor of fish, rare meat, fresh steamed vegetables and delicate flavors. A *cuisine nouvelle* dish looks very elegant when presented, but as with all new movements it has gone a little too far, and many of the dishes are often insubstantial. Besides, as with the wine, French cooking really falls into two main areas, the regional and the classical.

Regional cooking is by no means restricted to the regions. You will find restaurants offering regional food in Paris and all the major cities, while many regional dishes have now rightly gained a place on classical menus, but they are usually at their best when eaten in their native area, with the help of a local wine. I can think of few dishes better than a *ficelle picard,* a hot pancake of cheese and leeks from Picardy, or a Basque dish, *jambon piperade,* consisting of eggs, bacon and peppers, when served at the Hotel des Pyrénées in St Jean-Pied-de-Port. In the Beaujolais it has to be a good, rich, *coq-au-vin,* in Roussillon a *cargolade* of snails, along the Mediterranean coast a *soupe de poisson,* or a good *langouste.* Try the oysters from Cancale in Brittany, the trout of the Jura, a cheese dish, *raclette,* from Haute Savoie, or one of those delicious cheeses from Roquefort, Camembert or Brie, or a hundred others, which round off any meal before the fruit and the *tarte maison* are offered. After that you will need your *digestif,* from Cognac or Armagnac, or, if in Normandy, a glass of Calvados, apple brandy, for the *trou normand,* the 'Norman hole', before you feel really comfortable again.

As for the classic dishes, these tend to

Below A Paris winter market displays a wide range of produce, in spite of the weather.

Left This *epicier* offers a wide selection of French food: hams, patés, sausages, pies – all delicious.

Below Only the freshest and richest local produce finds a place in the Auvergnat charcuterie.

come in the main from Normandy, Burgundy or the Périgord, and are based on the three regional specialities of cream, wine and, from Périgord, truffles. To find dishes from these places, like *poisson beurre blanc,* a *côte de veau au pays d'Auge,* a *fricassée de volaille de Bresse,* you must consult the guides or on any evening in any town worth the name, go out about seven o'clock and wander around the streets. Find a small, rather well-lit restaurant, where the tables are filling up rapidly with local people and consult the menus displayed outside. If they serve local dishes, each a classic of its kind, enter at once to get a table. It may well be the meal of a lifetime.

Below The goose is one of the greatest attractions of the cuisine of Périgord.

Left Found deep in the woods, and gathered slowly by hand, wild mushrooms or *cepes* are a popular delicacy.

Below The waters of Vichy offer a 'cure' to those who have over-indulged in rich French cuisine.

Facing page It is possible to dine cheaply and well in small provincial cafés.

Left The ideal French picnic. Cheese, bread, wine, sunshine and a glorious view.

Below Coffee or an aperitif at a sidewalk café is a French institution.

Right A good wine and a great plate of escargots are the start of many French meals.

Far right French food and wine may be enjoyed in the cool and elegant surroundings in the very heart of Paris.

Below This *brigade* is outside the famous doors of Maxim's; a score of chefs are needed to prepare the finest haute cuisine.

Things to see in France

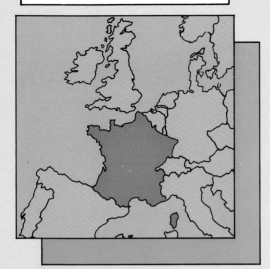

Loire Valley

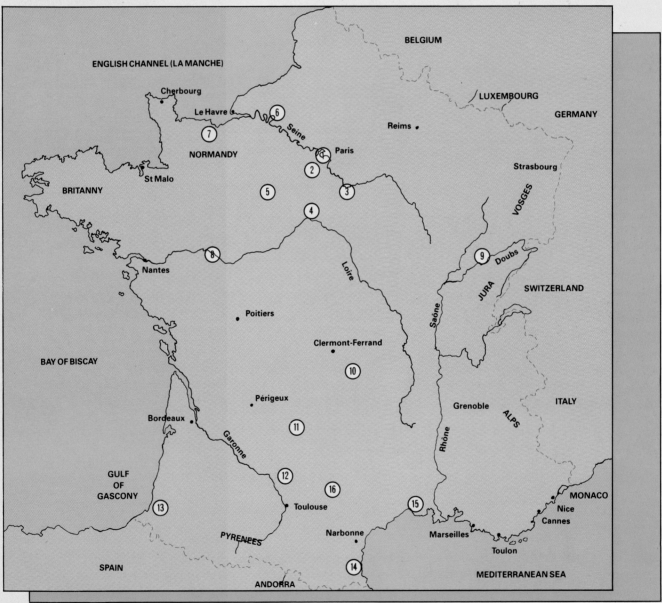

BELGIUM

ENGLISH CHANNEL (LA MANCHE)

LUXEMBOURG

GERMANY

Cherbourg

Le Havre ⑥

⑦ Seine

Reims

NORMANDY

Paris

Strasbourg

② ③

St Malo

⑤

BRITANNY

④

VOSGES

⑧

⑨ Doubs

Nantes

Loire

JURA

SWITZERLAND

Poitiers

Saône

BAY OF BISCAY

Clermont-Ferrand

⑩

Grenoble

ITALY

Périgeux

ALPS

Bordeaux

⑪

Garonne

Rhône

⑫

⑯

GULF
OF
GASCONY

⑮

MONACO

⑬

Toulouse

Nice

Cannes

PYRENEES

Narbonne

Marseilles

Toulon

SPAIN

⑭

MEDITERRANEAN SEA

ANDORRA

Fontainebleau

Orléans

Biarritz

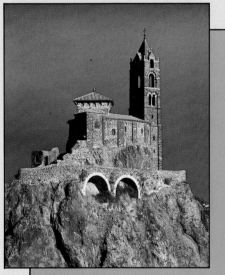
Auvergne

Sarlat

1. Paris
The heart of France, where all that is modern and sophisticated about the French nation rubs shoulders with countless monuments and leftovers from a fascinating history. Paris richly deserves its reputation as a world center of culture and the arts.

2. Versailles
Seat of the French court before the French revolution, this is one of Europe's most splendid palaces. Originally it was Louis XIII's hunting lodge.

3. Fontainebleau
Of all the French châteaux, Fontainebleau is the richest in historical links, dating back to Louis VII in the twelfth century. Beautiful gardens surrounded by a very large forest.

4. Orléans
A very splendid town on the Loire where at least two millenia of history have taken their colorful course. Joan of Arc, the Maid of Orléans, routed the English Army here in 1429.

5. Chartres
Setting for one of the grandest Gothic cathedrals in the world, Chartres is at the center of a fertile agricultural region known as the Beauce.

6. Rouen
This was a flourishing town even before the Romans came, and deserves fame for its magnificent Gothic cathedral.

7. Caen
Capital of Normandy under William the Conqueror, Caen is a fine northern town that has been immaculately rebuilt after extensive damage in the Second World War.

8. Loire Valley
At least a week should be set aside for visiting the Loire châteaux, and a month would be more realistic. Many of the châteaux have sophisticated *son et lumière* displays.

9. Besançon
One of France's most picturesque towns on a bend in the River Doubs amid the dramatic hilly scenery of Franche-Comté.

10. Auvergne
The volcanic landscape of the Auvergne in the Massif Central is a beautiful part of France, yet it is often overlooked by foreign visitors.

11. Sarlat
Just one delightful example of the Dordogne's beautiful towns, Sarlat can be explored in a leisurely fashion – you can walk all round it in a little over an hour.

12. Moissac
A fine example of the 'hidden' France: in this quiet southwestern town near the green valley of the River Lot stands the church of St Pierre, with its marvelously carved west door and cloisters.

13. Biarritz
Flanked by the Gulf of Gascony and a beach that is matchless for its surfing, Biarritz is a town with a difference, acquired in its more fashionable days before the 1930s.

14. Perpignan
A golden city of the Rousillon, Perpignan is the capital of French Catalonia – a region extending across the border into nearby Spain.

15. Aigues-Mortes
With plenty of picturesque remains – once it was a major rallying-point for the Crusades – Aigues-Mortes is today a starting-place for visits to the Camargue and its splendid wildlife.

16. Albi
Famous for its art gallery where paintings by Albi-born artist Toulouse-Lautrec are exhibited together with over 200 works by his contemporaries, this is a pleasant, airy town on the River Tarn.

Olive nets spread under the trees to catch the
falling crop.

PICTURE CREDITS